THEATER OF EXHIBITIONS

JENS HOFFMANN

Sternberg Press

The expansion of artistic practices throughout the twentieth century forged a path into today's interdisciplinary understanding of art and culture. Beginning with the early avant-gardists of the last century who looked around and saw the world radically changed, and advocated for an altered artistic practice to mirror their new surroundings, incorporating movement, sound, and self into their expressions; to the pioneers of the postwar era who forcefully placed the artist's body at the center of a dialogue that questioned the very limits of art and life; to today's discussions about the making, meaning, and distribution of images in the digital age. The once hard-and-fast lines that existed between the various disciplines have now dissolved in the post-medium era. One of the most important changes is perhaps the corrosion between formerly distinct spheres: the proscenium and the museum, the black box and the white cube, the theater and the street. Written from the point of view of a curator, this book considers these developments, examining how curators stand in dialogue with the newly formed practice of exhibition making in the twentieth and twenty-first centuries, which has adopted theatrical strategies and devises them in many ways. Theater here refers to the historical art form in which live performers present an imaginary or real event in front of an audience in a particular place, from ancient Greek drama to modern Western theater, such as that of Bertolt Brecht or Samuel Beckett.

In the context of this publication the term "theater" also refers to the spectacle and drama of the contemporary art world, to its often contrived and artificial nature, as well as to its frequent self-importance. While some of my

comments about these changes might seem exaggerated—
and I am certainly making generalizations about things
that warrant more nuanced examination—it is a fact that
the context of art has altered significantly over the last
two decades. Art has lost much of its status as a field of
intellectual ambition and political opposition or resistance
because of the overabundance of art and art schools,
and the emphasis placed on the importance of the art
market. Add to this the digital factor and we are clearly
looking at the emergence of an entirely new landscape
of contemporary, creative production. Whether these
developments are good or bad is not the main concern.
The sooner we accept that a change is underfoot, the sooner
we will be able to understand what art might look like
after the end of traditional notions of art and how this will
affect everyone working in the field. Some parts of this
book, based on previously published texts, function as
departure points for more in-depth examinations of a wide
range of subjects regarding theater and curating and their
relationship to today's art world that is full of challenges,
as well as opportunities. Art as we know it, specifically
modern and contemporary art, is a historical phenomenon
of the twentieth century; eventually something else will step
into its place that will critically, fearlessly, and beautifully
investigate what it means to be alive today.

SOME REMARKS ON:
THE END OF ART

When the American author William S. Burroughs
was asked to define art, he replied that art is a three-letter
word. As a poet, Burroughs was clearly a man of words
and fascinated by their meanings. While trying to point out
that a word is not the thing it represents, his answer also
describes a particular form of relativism that was key to
twentieth-century art. This relativism allowed art to open up
beyond the practices of painting and sculpture, shifting the
focus from the object to the concept. Yet by doing so this also
made it more difficult to clearly formulate the meaning and
possible boundaries of art, or how to measure its quality.

The Canadian media theorist Marshall McLuhan
probably summed it up the best when he stated, "Art is
anything you can get away with."[1] Today, art takes on such
diverse forms that it is almost impossible to define
stylistically; its systems of distribution and reception are
so varied, and reasons for making it are so different, that
the word "art" can really mean anything at all. However,
we continue to try to define this increasingly moving target.
Perhaps instead of talking about the definition, de-definition
or un-definition, or the end of art, we should ask what
remains at stake in maintaining the concept of art itself.

Since its beginnings, art has been concerned with its
own definition, and its unstable boundaries have progressively
deteriorated. Paradoxically, a work of art needs to be recog-
nizable as art before it can stray from the norm. It might
be argued that the value of an artwork in relationship to
the history of art lies in the balance between how much
it affirms or deviates from an existing canon. In the 1979
essay "Sculpture in the Expanded Field," which established

a new critical art-historical methodology, Rosalind Krauss
traces the genealogy of sculpture from Auguste Rodin
to 1960s and '70s American Land art.[2] While modernist
forms of sculpture negated the concept of site (a Brancusi
is an autonomous object), Krauss situates contemporary
sculpture—namely, Minimalist and Land art—at a nexus
between landscape and architecture. The work cannot be
removed from its site.

The biggest take from Krauss's text, however, is the
idea that old forms of defining sculpture are no longer valid,
and that the criteria for evaluation must be set through the
internal language of the work of art. While this methodology
radically opened up the field of art history so that the interpretation of an artwork defied traditional medium specificity,
it also makes all-encompassing statements on the status of
the art object impossible to understand.

When a word's meaning expands to this degree, when
almost any form of creative action can fit within its reach,
what does it do? While art's death has been proclaimed
countless times, the call to reconsider the viability of art
has become couched in more nuanced rhetoric. Perhaps the
term has outlived its usefulness. We should look for another
term that describes more adequately the totality of creative
production when we consider aesthetic (but also social and
political) gestures.

Making art has always entailed taking risks, challenging
expectations and established practices, and doing away with
the old. Today, dinner parties and garage sales are seen as
artworks, and they sit easily alongside traditional (and some
would say old-fashioned) painting and sculpture. Artists
are creating increasingly complex ecologies for their work,
seamlessly merging the symbolic system of art and the more
tangible systems of production and distribution. For example,

real estate is central to the conceptual practices of artists
like Rick Lowe and Theaster Gates. Rirkrit Tiravanija,
Minerva Cuevas, and Jon Rubin all established restaurants
as part of their work. Most recently, Tania Bruguera has
set up an immigrant community center in Corona Heights,
Queens, New York, and the collective Transformazium is
running a public library on the outskirts of Pittsburgh.
These projects suggest a radical departure from more
conventional forms of art, but perhaps more importantly,
they also break from traditional ways of experiencing and
understanding the artwork.

 These actions might mean and do more without
the weight and complexity of art history or traditional
definitions of art to burden them. The question that
arises, however, is will the work still be considered art?
One definition of art lies in the artist's intention: the work
of art is a work of art because an artist deems it so. This
definition quickly falls into a chicken-and-egg scenario.
Is it a work of art because an artist made it, and if so, what
constitutes an artist? Another defining characteristic of art
is the longstanding Kantian idea of art's purposelessness—
the idea that it does not need to meet certain ends or match
certain metrics to be considered of value. In fact, the more
rules it breaks, the more likely we are to consider it art.

 Even in its current form, art tests the rules of the
fields it consumes, never quite becoming the same as that
which it critiques. Art can astonish, surprise, or amaze,
but it can also shock and overwhelm, all the while
maintaining a distance, sitting a space apart. And that space
gives us the opportunity to think about what we do and
who we are in ways we would not if artists were primarily
concerned with efficiency and usefulness. When something
is considered art, this is a signal to pay attention in a

particular kind of way. It requests a readiness for the viewer
to take what is seen and apply it broadly, allowing art to
reverberate beyond its direct consequences.

There is no sense patrolling the boundaries of art
to keep certain things out—it is in art's nature to expand
beyond our perception of it. The exhibition, too, can be
as pliable and expansive as art is. It can stretch and sway
to accommodate the urgent arguments that need to be
made at any point in time. To make these arguments, it is
often necessary to look outside the context of art into
other relevant fields. A work might speak most clearly when
paired with historical ephemera or viewed through the
lens of a novel. Displaying an artwork alongside a related
but distinct counterpart can increase the impact of both—
the radical uselessness of the artwork sometimes speaks
most clearly when situated next to the most mechanical
and pointedly useful of things. As a museum professional
I am interested in these questions to understand how
aesthetic gestures will continue to express themselves, how
curators try to mediate those gestures to an ever-growing
public, and what the role and function of an art institution
is today and in the future.

While many everyday products have clear benchmarks
and systems for assessment, these objective standards are
elusive when it comes to art and curatorial production.
Assessing a thing's quality involves measuring its excellence
in comparison to other things of a similar kind. If a model
is in flux, so are its standards. As art travels further afield from
traditional ideas, variables increase and assessment becomes
more and more difficult. How do we assess the quality of
an idea? Without a measure of quality a field cannot advance,
or so it seems, and forward movement proves difficult when
the field is expanding outward into a number of directions.

Do we judge a work modeled after a dinner party against other such events, even if it challenges the very form it adopts? And could it be assessed against other artworks oriented in the social sphere? What about aesthetic, ethical, and moral standards? What about the participants of these projects? How are they different from or equal to the artists? We find ourselves swimming among forms and methods, and the benchmarks are set adrift. Alongside this confusion, there is also a tendency to accept new forms, bloating the field without hesitation in order to appear progressive. Rather than risk appearing to impose judgment, curators want to be seen as benevolent facilitators, advocating for all artists rather than making a strong case for a few. An exhibition need not only be a showcase or indiscriminate sampling of new art. It can be a crucial space to take a position on the status of art today, creating an argument through the carefully considered juxtaposition of works in a space.

Too often, part of this curatorial oversight means a disregard of the crucial element of context. To look only at a finished art product is to ignore the conditions of production and reception that make a work possible. To consider only a diamond's color, clarity, and size is to ignore the systemic warfare and economic disparity its production and distribution are rooted in. Further, any discussion of the meaning or quality of art also deals with another, similarly contentious issue: taste. Taste, even in today's populist environment of citizen bloggers and top-ten lists, implies a high level of education and ample leisure time. If we are honest, such subjectivities play a part in many curatorial decisions. Museums often have collection management policies to guide the accession and deaccession of works, but while *quality* is a word used frequently in such documents, it is rarely if ever defined. The process of assessment inevitably involves subjective considerations. The existing canon is one of the only operative benchmarks to evaluate a new work, and it was built through various decisions of taste.

While there is discussion about what curating does today, I still consider the exhibition as the primary curatorial product, a discursive argument realized through the display of artworks. The format is time-tested but still new, centuries old but full of possibility. The peculiarities of the exhibition as a unique social ritual are myriad. Its making involves elements of staging and theatricality, and its viewing is likewise a performance, whether it entails treading silently through a white cube, willingly giving oneself over to the things presented, or encountering an unusual arrangement in a familiar environment. The exhibition can be used to suspend disbelief as one does with a piece of fiction. The exhibition format is built for a particular kind of collective activity. It allows for a sense of being alone together—to be part of a shared experience.

For many institutions and galleries, programming has supplanted the exhibition format at the center. In the name of innovation, many curators have abandoned exhibition making in favor of other forms, among them screenings, conversations, roundtables, lecture series, residencies, publications, meetings, and workshops. As opposed to the exhibition, which is bound inextricably—and productively—to the artifice of art, these forms are perceived to be the stuff of real life, and there is a strong desire to utilize their perceived authenticity. Such programs are equipped to draw in larger audiences rather than more traditional arrangements presumed to be static. Participation and interaction have come to have more currency than observation and introspection. The exhibition can be a vital way to slow down or suspend time, allowing us to think more carefully about the world in which we exist and the role art can play in illuminating our human condition.

In the rush to explore social forms as venues for art making and curating, it is easy to forget that the exhibition is such a form—one that remains rich in untapped promise. It can fit within it every other discipline, appropriating the fields of science, architecture, theater, or television, to name a few. To abandon the transformative power of the exhibition prematurely is cynical and suggests that its possibilities have been exhausted. But it is important to make a distinction between advocating for a longstanding form and freezing it in a past or current state. When we consider the form as a significant social ritual, we must acknowledge that society is not static. As society changes, so must the exhibition, and the form of the exhibition should meet the public halfway. To say that curating should remain fundamentally about exhibition making is not to say that exhibition making should stay the same, or even that it can.

SOME REMARKS ON:
ART AFTER THE END OF ART

If it is true that every era in history gets the art it deserves, we are not in a particularly good period. It has been a long time since a traditional contemporary art exhibition has had a strong effect on me. I feel a certain fatigue regarding art made today, and I often enjoy looking at and examining historical works or even nonart objects and materials from cultural history much more. The thought that art is dead is not a new idea; critics and writers have declared the death of art repeatedly. The title for this section of the book was inspired by Arthur C. Danto's essay "The End of Art" (1984), which speaks about art's status and role in a post-historical age.[3] Another important contribution to this discussion was clearly Hans Belting's "The End of the History of Art?" (1983), in which he argued that more and more contemporary art was conscious of past art but was not moving art forward—thus art had become an eternal spiral of recycling, mixing, and appropriating.[4] Danto and Belting made various revisions to their texts and expanded on their ideas over the years, building up an enormous arsenal of supporting arguments. For both, a major historical shift was taking place in the early 1980s, resulting from a form of internal exhaustion within a grand narrative of art history that was then neatly divided into ancient, medieval, and modern periods, having not yet undergone the drastic changes the 1990s would bring: the globalization of the art world and discourses around post-colonialism, identity politics, and even post-structuralism. More recently art historian David Joselit's *After Art* (2012) looks at developments in art and architecture in the age of digital search engines, and the enormous acceleration

of cultural production whereby artists and architects function more and more like information hubs of larger creative networks than actual producers of content.[5]
A further book I should highlight, and one that is a little removed from the debates found in the previous publications mentioned, is Rasheed Araeen's *Art Beyond Art* (2011) in which the author speaks about practices that have a self-understanding of art but manage to avoid being seen as art within what he calls the "legitimizing prison house" of bourgeois aesthetics.[6]

Art has never existed autonomously but is always part of a larger cultural context, shaped by the political, social, and economic conditions of its time. Art is a product of its surroundings and in an ideal situation, comments on or at least reflects on the circumstances that shape it. Making art is one way to seek answers to fundamental questions of human existence. Not that art could ever produce answers to these questions, but each artwork can be understood as a piece of a big puzzle, illuminating the significance of life, human thought, and the world around us.

After talking with some of my close colleagues in the field of exhibition making, it seems I am not the only one who is experiencing this lethargy toward contemporary art, which on particularly bad days can even be called disillusionment. Many curators have abandoned the idea of making exhibitions altogether, and instead organize conferences or publish books that directly address social and political circumstances; others look at art made by so-called nonartists or outsiders; some prefer to work more and more with historical art, or view contemporary art as only one of various areas that can offer discourse and materials for exhibitions, looking also to architecture, film, fashion, design, and other areas of cultural production.

Maybe curators ask too much from artists. Perhaps it is perfectly fine to simply enjoy a conversation about the evolution of abstract painting in Latin America, minute details of Eastern European Minimalism, or hyper-theorized Conceptual art, but in the long run art should be part of something larger and more significant than personal taste. Art should move us toward social justice. How can we achieve that without robbing art of the autonomy it has acquired in the modern era? What makes matters more complicated if not worse is the self-importance of a lot of contemporary art (as well as the context that surrounds it). The insularity of the art world and its ignorance regarding other practices and fields is frustrating and painful.

While art as we know it has been around for over seven hundred years, the way we look at art and artists is a product of the twentieth century. What if the twentieth century's idea of art and its concept of the artist no longer existed? What if we continue to keep those ideas alive when they have in fact become obsolete? What if art is no longer the radically creative and intellectual field we always thought it to be, and has regressed to be nothing more than a shadow of its former self?

A shift is taking place in how we understand and judge art, and this change affects curating and exhibition making. This is different from the shift that Belting, Danto, and even Joselit spoke about—it is now the result of a number of rather recent events and processes.

First, there is the almost conveyor-belt fabrication of tens of thousands of aspiring artists per year in Master of Fine Arts programs around the world. The advantages and disadvantages of this form of education have been debated at length and I will not get into it much here, but art schools have become mills that produce hordes of often unexceptional artists who, for better or worse, might get a shot at a career in the art world if they're lucky but rarely contribute to the discourse around art. Their work, to put it drastically, pulls down the overall quality of what is being produced, reducing art to conceptual decoration, ready to be sold in a random gallery to collectors who match the works with the interior decor of their houses—and art ends up losing its integrity.

Art, or what many people believe to be art, has become a billion-dollar industry. While the commodification of art is not new, the level of financial power operating in the art world now is unprecedented, and so is the impact of this development on the progress of art. That there is serious money to be made in the art world has changed the rules of the game dramatically and irreversibly. There is now an enormous art market with million-dollar auction records and hundreds of art fairs that need objects for sale, offering art as if it were merchandise. In addition, there is an ever-increasing community of contemporary art galleries around the world, many of which do excellent work and many of which do not—but all must constantly show and sell art to keep their spaces running.

The fact that many museums have turned into tourist attractions and entertainment centers is another development to consider, as audience figures become the main focus for directors, boards, and curators. Risk-taking exhibitions that articulate a passionate point of view, or take a stand on a political or social subject are few and far between. The alliances made between art dealers, museum patrons (most often art collectors), and the institutions are frightening and often full of conflicting interests. Given the enormous amount of art produced today, it is becoming difficult for museums to determine what to collect and how to judge the overall quality of art. The classic role of the museum as an archive that is significant to the development of art is passé. Even the most provincial museums in the West have realized that the narrative arc they have created in their collections is, in most cases, based on a Eurocentric worldview. Including art from the so-called margins—art made by artists from contexts previously excluded from the conversation and fields previously deemed uncollectable—is of course not the only change that museums must undergo.

The concept of a linear development of art, a straight and resolved historical master narrative, is itself incredibly flawed, and for the most part has been discredited and overcome. Questioning the idea of a linear narrative of art and history and the idea of canon building challenges the traditional reason behind the existence of museums, as well as the story of art as we know it—art that is made in a studio, exhibited in a gallery, sold to a museum, stored, analyzed, conserved, and displayed. While these narratives seem to help (some of) us form our (cultural) identity, making us feel rooted and secure, they are most often simply subjective and speculative, serving only to affirm existing social and cultural hierarchies and moribund power dynamics.

Why museums continue to buy contemporary art in traditional ways should be contested given the type of art and the amount of art produced these days. Collecting art that has a permanent importance should be priority; it is the foundation of why we collect in the first place. When it comes to art created today, the relevance is highly temporary—this is antithetical to the whole idea of collecting as many works lose their meaning in a very short time. As a result, the relationships between art, art making, and museums have irreversibly changed. Art has taken on a life of its own, and is often disconnected from the outside world. Given the focus on temporary exhibitions and event-oriented programming in most museums, it seems as if collecting contemporary art is, and maybe should be, a thing of the past. Museums, however, should continue to collect historical works that hold permanent importance in the history of art. What seems unclear, given their original mission, is why museums chase every new trend in today's fluctuating contemporary art scene.

On top of all this, the digital world we now live in is changing the relationship between art and ourselves more dramatically than anything else. While most online art projects still hang on to the idea of art as object or concept, transferring and translating those thoughts onto the Internet, the impact the digital world will ultimately have on our understanding of art cannot be underestimated. In many ways the original work of art has become secondary to the image of it. The majority of people encounter art today in the form of digital images found on websites, in e-mails, or via social media. This is only the beginning. What makes digital art so engaging but also so challenging is that it has no rules, no confines, no standards, no systems, and no laws. There is no standardized format for its presentation, unlike sculptures and paintings made for a white-cube environment. Digital art has not yet found a common form, and I doubt it will. While it is blessing to find a truly open forum for art, it will also be difficult for us to assess it.

SOME REMARKS ON:
THE ALLEGED DEATH OF THE EXHIBITION

The word curator has become diluted. In contemporary usage it too often means selecting and choosing in any context—for instance, the selection of music by a DJ in a club, the selection of menu items in a restaurant, or the act of decorating a shop window in a fancy department store. I prefer to define the curator as a "maker of exhibitions." Exhibition making is the creation of a display within a particular sociopolitical space, with a carefully formulated argument presented through the meticulous selection and methodical installation of artworks, related objects from the sphere of art, and objects from other areas of visual culture.

By and large, however, new tendencies in curating have become less about exploring novel models of exhibition making and more about overcoming the idea of exhibition making altogether, focusing instead on film screenings, lecture series, performances, educational events, artistic and curatorial residencies, and publications. In some cases, the "death of the exhibition" has already been proclaimed by those who maintain that innovation in the field can only happen if more "flexible" forms of presentation are sought.

Yet the exhibition remains to be the primary space for encountering art. There is a huge diversity of exhibition formats available to explore. We have only scratched the surface. Exhibitions still offer many untapped possibilities in how artists and curators mediate content that is artistic, political, or cultural. The focus on exhibitions as the main platform to experience art and culture, to disseminate and mediate artistic and intellectual concepts, and to produce knowledge is perhaps becoming unfashionable among the curatorial intelligentsia. But I have no investment in the academic notion of "the curatorial" as a strategy to bypass art or exhibitions. This methodology of the curatorial, made well known by Irit Rogoff and the PhD curating program at Goldsmiths, University of London, defines curating as a nebulous variety of cultural and artistic practices that fuses a wide range of activities, such as teaching, activism, discourse production, as well as art making, with little or no regard for exhibition making as a craft.[7]

On the other end of the spectrum, many museums and biennials have turned into a sector of the entertainment industry, as sites for the delivery of experiences and social gatherings rather than the provision of education and reflection. The truth is that art is not for everyone, and only a small fraction of society is really interested. Are attempts to draw larger audiences really about bringing art to the people? Or are they superficial gestures, turning museums into tourist attractions or theme parks that are mostly relevant for marketing numbers?

The (sometimes overtly expressed) assumption is that to just show art is (at best) simplistic and (at worst) boring, and that there is a need for extensive public programs and other gimmicks, such as gigantic commissions à la Tate Modern, music concerts, or performance spectacles to keep audiences excited and coming back. While many of these additional programs originated from a well-meant desire to present art forms that could not be shown in the galleries and to provide a context for exhibitions on view, such programming has taken on a life of its own.

It is unsurprising that a static display of art objects could be perceived as insufficient or not dynamic enough, since the exhibition does not necessarily enable social interaction and requires not only patience but also effort on the part of the audience to engage with seemingly difficult artistic and curatorial arguments. That is not to say exhibitions should not be entertaining. But surely they should not only be *entertainment*. Looking at a well-curated exhibition should be an effort. It should be an educational, intellectually stimulating, inspiring experience.

I should clarify that much of my criticism is directed toward larger museums using non-exhibition-centered programming purely as a means to attract bigger audiences. Smaller institutions that are less audience-focused and more intellectually and politically minded are using non-exhibition-based curatorial efforts to "academicize" and "theorize" curating, which has its own advantages and disadvantages

Catherine David's documenta X (1997) was a prime example of an exhibition whose accompanying program, "100 Days – 100 Guests," enabled productive, multi-disciplinary academic discourse outside the exhibition space.[8] Following the idea of documenta as the "museum of 100 days," each evening a different paper was presented by one of the one hundred invited participants, which included filmmakers, anthropologists, psychoanalysts, writers, philosophers, economists, and architects. Okwui Enwezor's documenta XI (2002) pushed this idea even further with five satellite symposia, the "Platforms," which took place in Vienna, Berlin, Lagos, St. Lucia, and New Delhi.[9]

Expanded programming is now a core element of any art institution. Seminars and the publication of academic materials have become standard, often replacing traditional catalogues. Another recent trend has been the investigation of new pedagogical modes and alternative education models within the walls of the museum, such as temporary schools, evening workshops, weekend seminars, and traveling libraries. The trick, as I see it, is not to abandon the idea of exhibition making too soon but to continually seek new

forms within it. Let's relinquish the tired categories of
solo, mid-career, group, historical survey, and so on,
striving instead for the personal and quixotic, as well as
the academically rigorous.

The curator Ute Meta Bauer is an excellent example
of someone who takes a hybrid approach, integrating archival
and visual material into a structure that is part exhibition,
part arena for intellectual exchange and political debate,
while not at all turning away from the idea of an exhibition
as a forum for the display of art objects. Her exhibition "?,"
which was part of the now-legendary exhibition "NowHere"
(1996) at the Louisiana Museum outside Copenhagen,
stands out as an early example of a more theoretically inclined
method of exhibition making.[10] For this one-time experiment,
the permanent collection was placed into storage, and the
entire museum was handed over to four independent curators
to demonstrate the diversity of contemporary curatorial
positions. Meta Bauer was one of the international curators
invited by the former director of the museum, Lars Nittve.
"NowHere" incorporated institutional critical thinking into
the curatorial process and analyzed exhibitions as social events
by trying to examine the history of the venue as a bastion
of humanist and liberal yet elitist and bourgeois ideology.
While the exhibition was not perceived as a success—
it perhaps broke too radically with traditional exhibition
formats—it was a valuable early experiment attempting
a dialogue with more discourse-oriented artistic practices.

Swiss curator Hans Ulrich Obrist, who began his
career in the mid-1990s, single-handedly revolutionized
curating. He certainly owed much of his creative impulses
to the more unorthodox curators working in the 1970s and
1980s (Harald Szeemann, Johannes Cladders, Walter Hopps,
Lucy Lippard, Jan Hoet, Kasper König, and Pontus Hultén,

to mention a few), and vehemently supported the idea of looking at artworks in relation to other disciplines, connecting the display of artworks to architecture, filmmaking, literature, and science. He presented exhibitions in unusual locations, such as the houses of historically important architects and writers, his kitchen, a hotel room, and relied heavily on audience participation. In exhibitions such as the ongoing "Do It," which began in 1993, the audience is allowed to realize artworks and exhibitions using instructions written by well-known artists.[11] As of late, Obrist has moved away from the exhibition as the main focus of his curatorial undertakings and centers his activities more on publishing, in particular on his interview project and the conversation marathons. A lot of the innovative work done by exhibition makers in mainstream art institutions since 2000 owes much to the ideas Obrist first introduced, even though he himself is now focused on other areas of cultural production.

Innovation has also come from the involvement of artists in the curatorial process, especially in the arena of collection displays. This trend, consistently cited by curators, is a way to "think past" the confines of an institutional collection. I will mention two historical examples because they have been incredibly influential for so many curators. Joseph Kosuth's "The Play of the Unmentionable" (1990), organized at the Brooklyn Museum, looked at how art has been censored in different cultures throughout the ages.[12] Kosuth selected and displayed one hundred artworks from the museum's collections—African, Middle Eastern, Classical, Asian, Prints and Drawings, et cetera—that had been censored by public officials or religious institutions at some point. The second is Fred Wilson's "Mining the Museum" (1992) at the Maryland Historical Society in Baltimore.[13] As an artist in residence for a year prior to the show, Wilson extensively studied the art, artifacts, and archives in the historical society, and discovered many artifacts related to suppressed minority histories in the United States. Treating the collection as what he called "raw materials," he deconstructed and rearranged it to expose how the museum systematically represented (or more often failed to represent) histories of African Americans and Native Americans.

There are three more—very different and idiosyncratic but highly innovative—makers of exhibitions that must be mentioned here. The first is the independent art space Triple Candie (now in Philadelphia but originally located for a decade in Harlem, New York). Since its inception in 2001, it has become a stronghold of curatorial innovation, particularly with their "exhibitions about art without art." Two such exhibitions include "David Hammons: The Unauthorized Retrospective" (2006), which was realized via photocopies and computer printouts without the artist's approval, and "Cady Noland Approximately: Selected Work, 1984–2000" (2006), the first survey of Cady Noland's art, consisting of thirteen sculptural approximations built using incomplete information gathered on the Internet.[14] Both exhibitions were highly controversial for disregarding the intentions of the artists whose work was on display. At the same time, the art space introduced a number of innovations, such as new ways to organize radical exhibitions without much of a budget.

The second is the formerly Toronto-based curator, collector, artist, scholar, and philanthropist Ydessa Hendeles, who curated some of the most unusual but extremely inspiring combinations of high-caliber artworks and contemporary and historical nonart materials. Her work has fortunately received increased attention over the last few years, yet only a small handful of people have had the privilege of seeing her exhibitions in person. With such shows as "The Teddy Bear Project" (2002), "Partners" (2003), "Predators and Prey" (2006), and "Dead! Dead! Dead!" (2007), Hendeles has pushed radical, subjective curating to an entirely new level.[15] "The Teddy Bear Project," which juxtaposed thousands of photographs of teddy bears with a sculpture of Hitler by Maurizio Cattelan, highlighted very intimate episodes of Hendeles's life, in particular her experiences as a child in Germany born to Holocaust survivors. "Dead! Dead! Dead!" was loosely organized around the traditional British puppet show featuring Punch and Judy. Hendeles combined a large selection of historical Punch and Judy puppets, a collection of Joan Crawford's charm bracelets, and Victorian-era billy clubs, alongside artworks by Charles Ray, James Coleman, Thomas Schütte, Louise Bourgeois, Marcel Dzama, and others to create a complex collage that spoke eloquently about violence, death, power, discontent, frustration, and class society.

Finally, Philippe Parreno's impressive and highly theatrical exhibition "Anywhere, Anywhere Out of the World" took place at the Palais de Tokyo in 2013, and understood the exhibition as a medium in its own right, continuing the long engagement of artists with the concept of the exhibition as a work of art staged not unlike a theatrical experience via interaction with the architecture of the site, and the inclusion of such traditional theater devices such as music, light, and props, as well as film and the actual (permanent) performance of objects and people.[16] While envisioned as a retrospective, the exhibition turned into a dramatic experience that would offer the viewer an opportunity to walk through the career of the artist, looking at old and new works of art, and artworks by other artists Parreno has close affinities with (such as Liam Gillick or Dominique Gonzalez-Foerster). The gallery space is turned into a theatrical stage—the collaborative effort of Parreno, his colleagues, the audience, the building, as well as the intellectual structure of the institution it took place in.

These and other examples of groundbreaking excellence from the last decade not only reveal that the art exhibition is alive and well, but that there is still an enormous amount of work to be done. I wonder what would have happened in the last twenty years if curators had put less effort into expanding and diversifying what curating could mean outside the white cube, and more effort into radically examining what takes place within walls of the gallery space—a space to which I feel extremely dedicated. Making exhibitions is necessary, not only for the presentation of artworks, but also as a very particular mode of rendering intellectual thinking in a creative, visual, and experiential way.

SOME REMARKS ON:
THE GALLERY AS THEATER

I am a curator, not a theorist or an art historian.
Specifically, my curatorial practice has always been based on
creating an experience for an audience, rather than situating
objects within particular art-historical narratives as museum
curators of the past generally thought of themselves to be
doing. I consider my practice an extended consideration of
what kind of experience can be created with art in the space
of an exhibition.

This impulse to create a lived experience through art
and exhibitions comes from a background in theater and an
interest in particular strands of critical theory. I was trained
as a theater director at the Ernst Busch Academy of Dramatic
Arts in Berlin where I was introduced to the theory and
practices of Bertolt Brecht and Erwin Piscator, as well as many
of the writings of the Frankfurt School. This sparked a lifelong
interest in the idea of fostering critical and political engagement with an audience through the staging of an experience.

In particular, influences have been Piscator's "epic
theater" (a term the better-known Brecht later borrowed),
which Piscator's wife, Maria Ley-Piscator, defined as "a theater
for vast audiences, a theater of action, whose objective is to
bring about the stirring questions of our time and to bring
about the total re-education of both men of the theater and
the audience."[17] She also said of his work: "It was as much
a political revolution as it was an aesthetic one."[18]

Epic theater worked toward portraying reality—
as opposed to fantasy or escapism—by employing certain
stage settings, acting techniques, and modes of interaction
that could ideally engender the ability to raise political
consciousness. Piscator was also the first theater director

to mix media, so to speak, by incorporating film into his productions. This is another aspect of his practice that has been relevant to my development as a curator.

I conceive of the exhibition as a stage set in which the objects on display are performers. Their interrelationships, and also the meanings these juxtapositions create for a viewer within a highly individualized and subjective time and space, are performers as well. In an ideal situation, the viewer becomes an additional performer within this dynamic, connecting their individual subjectivities and life experiences with the works in the exhibition to create even more new meanings. The exhibition, as a creative medium, establishes and cultivates a specific nexus between individuals and objects. The curator is the author of this nexus, selecting and installing the artworks, which as a group offer a larger argument than any one work could make by itself. The exhibition mirrors the subjectivity of the individual curator, just as each artwork mirrors the subjectivity of the artist who made it.

The work of Herbert Marcuse is especially relevant in thinking about this, in particular one of his last writings *The Aesthetic Dimension*, published in 1978, which is a critique of the orthodox Marxist view of art.[19] While Marcuse (like Walter Benjamin, Theodor Adorno, and the rest of the Frankfurt School) holds out for the radical potential of art to impact society at large, he takes a more inclusive approach. He does not dismiss art that does not reflect the modernization of society (Benjamin), or artworks that do not fit into the high avant-garde (Adorno). For Marcuse, the work of art can transcend particular class ideologies in which it was created, and can exist autonomously outside of those societal relations. In fact, he believes that the "political potential of art lies only in its own aesthetic dimension," and

in the subversive critical thinking that the work engenders—
what he calls estrangement.[20] Marcuse champions beauty and
form over all categories of art, high and low, and he decries
overly politically didactic work, claiming that it "deprives
art of the very form in which it can create that other reality
within the established one—the cosmos of hope."[21]

Subjectivity is a key component in Marcuse's analysis,
and it is something I always consider in my exhibitions—
both my own subjectivity as an exhibition maker and the
subjectivity of the viewer. This is not an "art for art's sake"
argument; those days are thankfully gone. Fundamentally,
it is about developing conditions for engendering critical
consciousness through art, as well as resisting the reduction
of art to practical ends. Subjectivity in this context can be
troubling—Marcuse himself acknowledges that subjectivity
is a capitalistic, bourgeois construction. At the same time,
subjectivity has become dominant in our epistemology,
the way we think about the world around us, and this
potentially makes it a challenging and "antagonistic force"
that can foster real change.

SOME REMARKS ON:
THE CURATOR AS AN AGENT
OF SOCIAL CHANGE

Epic theater has been described by Leo Kerz as
"a theater of awareness that could comment and communicate
beyond the linear progression and fragmentary story of the
page-play itself."[22] An exhibition, like theater, is a unique
format for thinking through ideas, history, and culture, and
a way to engender new forms of awareness of the world
around us. One can transform a supposedly neutral gallery
space into a microcosm of the world, and by making
exhibitions that are different from regular museum shows,
provoke the idea that we can all live differently based on an
awareness of our own thoughts, choices, and environment.

Social and political change is possible, but to achieve
this we must look back at history and analyze art and our
experience of it within a broader cultural framework. I think
that exhibitions are a great tool for education because they
allow every medium to be present—not only literature,
film, and performance, but also elements of cultural history.
I strongly believe in the idea of the total artwork toward
total education. Education through art is the central concept
and methodology of my practice. I do not make activist
exhibitions but I still consider myself a political curator.
I would say that I am a curator informed by a very particular
political position, and that my exhibitions are constructed
with this in mind, in both form and content.

I attempted to put these ideas explicitly into play in
the 12th Istanbul Biennial in 2011.[23] I was invited to curate
the biennial together with my longtime colleague Adriano
Pedrosa. We intended to explore the rich relationship
between art and politics, focusing on works that are both

30

formally innovative and politically outspoken. In this way, the exhibition not only followed a particular curatorial thread within the history of the Istanbul Biennial— a longing to connect art to the contemporary realities of the world—but also engaged in a dialogue with a recent series of exceedingly political biennial exhibitions around the globe in which aesthetic concerns had sometimes taken a backseat to the pressing political concerns of our time.

Pedrosa and I took as our conceptual point of departure the Cuban American artist Félix González-Torres, whose work is both politically provocative and rigorously attentive to the formal aspects of artistic production. The artist, a figure between North and South—specifically between Cuba, his place of birth, and the United States, his adopted home country—successfully negotiated the territory between the personal and the political while maintaining an extremely sophisticated formal vocabulary, utilizing an aesthetic language drawn in part from post-Minimalism and Conceptualism and in part from everyday life.

The title we chose for the biennial, *Untitled (12th Istanbul Biennial)*, 2011, deliberately referenced the way in which González-Torres named most of his works as *Untitled*, followed by a description in parentheses. It reflected González-Torres's idea that his artworks were untitled "because 'meaning' is always shifting in time and space."[24] For him, meaning was not a monolithic entity, but constantly in flux, and so our exhibition announced itself through its title as intentionally open to various forms of interpretation rather than dispensing a spoon-fed message.

Another approach toward exhibition making is to take literature as a departure point, to cast the curator as an author who, over the course of several shows or an entire career, presents a larger argument, articulates a particular worldview. It is a creative form of exhibition making, but no less rigorous than the art-historical methodologies of a more traditional curator. The curator is a kind of storyteller, translating the narrative of a book into the narrative of an exhibition, turning the viewer into a reader.

I have frequently invoked François Truffaut's iconic essay "A Certain Tendency of the French Cinema," first published in 1954, to describe my theory of curating.[25] The essay introduced the influential theory of the auteur and described a transformation happening in cinema at that time, whereby film directors sought to be perceived on the same creative level as literary authors. Truffaut's text, closely linked to the films of the Nouvelle Vague and French cinema of the 1950s, originated as a response to the Hollywood studio system and traditional forms of filmmaking in France. Transferring this argument into the context of today's visual-art world, the American film studios could be compared to large museums, and traditional filmmaking could be perceived as similar to curating a museum collection according to a standard chronological or art-genre categorization scheme.

For Truffaut, the characteristics of an author-director include thematic consistency of production, a strong creative sensibility regarding how the director interprets a script, and a clear artistic development from film to film throughout the director's career. All of these attributes could be applied to many curators working today. A clear paradigm shift in curating has taken place since the 1990s, and although it is too early to analyze the effects this change will have in the long term, it can safely be said that curating has reinvented itself to such a degree that it will never return to the situation in which the curator was perceived as facilitator or caretaker.

One cannot speak of the curator-as-author without taking into consideration one of the most important critiques of auteur theory: post-structuralism. Roland Barthes, for instance, formulated a rejection of this theory in his 1967 essay "The Death of the Author," arguing against the belief that the author is the sole unifying, creative source that gives meaning and value to a work of art.[26] This criticism has been widely accepted today. The manner in which I use the idea of the author in my practice fully considers and follows the idea of authorship as "a certain functional principle by which, in our culture, one limits, excludes, and chooses," as defined by Michel Foucault in his 1969 lecture "What Is an Author?"[27] The result of this selection process could be called a unique and novel creation, with the creative act being a result of the transformation of chaos into order— a selection from an infinite number of possibilities. This is ultimately how I would describe a curator: someone who limits, excludes, and creates meaning with existing signs, codes, and materials. Within the process of making an exhibition, the curator becomes somewhat decentered, only part of a larger structure. He or she holds a subject position, not always the core, despite occupying a more powerful distributive agency than some of the other elements or individuals in that structure.

Unsurprisingly, many curators responsible for this new understanding of curating have worked or work mostly outside of institutions—or at smaller and more flexible institutions that afford a large degree of independence. The advantages and disadvantages of working as an independent curator versus working for an institution have been discussed at length in the last few years. Let me say that being an independent curator—supposedly a very attractive profession—is in reality far from congenial. Only a handful of independent curators make a living from their earnings. Most are independent simply because they cannot find a stable position in an institution, rather than because they believe in the idea of independence in the true sense of the word, as a political principle.

It is possible that independent curating reached its peak with Francesco Bonami's Venice Biennale in 2003, where he divided the exhibition into ten sections, each one curated by different individuals. The focus on curating and curators in Bonami's show triggered much criticism, and it is fair to say in retrospect that this was the grand finale for the independent curator of the 1990s. While it was a celebration of diversity in curating (and one of the few occasions, perhaps, when the real differences among independent curatorial approaches were clearly apparent), one unfortunate result was that audiences began to grow tired of this kind of format, and large, very experimental group exhibitions started to become less popular, perceived as too specialized for broad audiences.

Is there any site, then, that still welcomes alternative approaches to curating? Over the last few years many intellectually and politically ambitious curators have moved into positions at smaller institutions. By "smaller" I mean artist-run or alternative spaces, nonprofit galleries, and university museums. Examples in the United States include Artists Space, New York; LAX Art, Los Angeles; Renaissance Society, Chicago; the Institute of Contemporary Art,

Philadelphia; MIT's List Visual Arts Center, Cambridge, Massachusetts; and the SculptureCenter, Long Island City, New York, to mention only a few. In Europe I would include Tensta konsthall, Stockholm; The Showroom, London; Kunsthalle Vienna; Van Abbemuseum, Eindhoven; SALT, Istanbul; Witte de With, Rotterdam; BAK, Utrecht; Le Consortium, Dijon, among many others.

Operating at this level has its origin, I believe, in the late 1960s when Harald Szeemann was the director of the Kunsthalle Bern in Switzerland, and revolutionized the art world with his groundbreaking 1969 exhibition "When Attitudes Become Form."[28] At these smaller institutions, curators can maintain high professional and intellectual standards while being allowed to take more experimental paths. They have the best of both worlds: stability and responsibility, and are motivated to find new ways to engage with their audiences.

Even the most conservative institutions by now understand that curating has changed, and many of them are inviting curators to organize exhibitions, albeit in relatively "safe" and contained ways. A major museum may demand experimentalism, but always in a palatable form, using the phenomenon of the "guest independent curator" as a way to simultaneously embrace and distance itself from truly experimental programming. We all know the priorities of most museums—audience figures and fundraising—and it will not come as a surprise that their exhibitions, therefore, are rarely allowed to be *too* radical. A curator in a large institution may often have no say in what I consider the fundamental parts of a show: the title, the exhibition catalogue cover, the press images, the schedule, even the exhibition content. Many of these tasks are now under the purview of PR, development, and marketing departments.

And there still remains the question of where the profession is headed in the next few decades. Will the trend be a return to independent curating, away from institutions of all sizes? A continued pursuit of biennial and triennial curating gigs in ever more remote corners of the world? Undoubtedly, if one is invested in the idea of exhibitions as manifestations of a personal creative vision, there are necessary conditions for that, such as control over the entire production process. So far, there is no system in place that comes with zero constraints—no truly free zone for creative curating. In general, exhibition making is directed toward a niche audience of art insiders. However, museums have been taken over by blockbuster exhibitions, and biennials are similarly controlled by their own web of complex constraints because of the politics of funding, audience figures, and so on.

As long as this continues, "authored" exhibition making will be a problematic business for curators. The goal must be to create intelligent shows with mass appeal. We need a system that will allow independent curators to find producers for their curatorial endeavors, inside and outside of institutions, in a manner similar to the author-directors of the 1950s, and to bring their projects to larger audiences. If communicated in the right way, specialized exhibitions might appeal to the wider public. But it may be a long time until we get there.

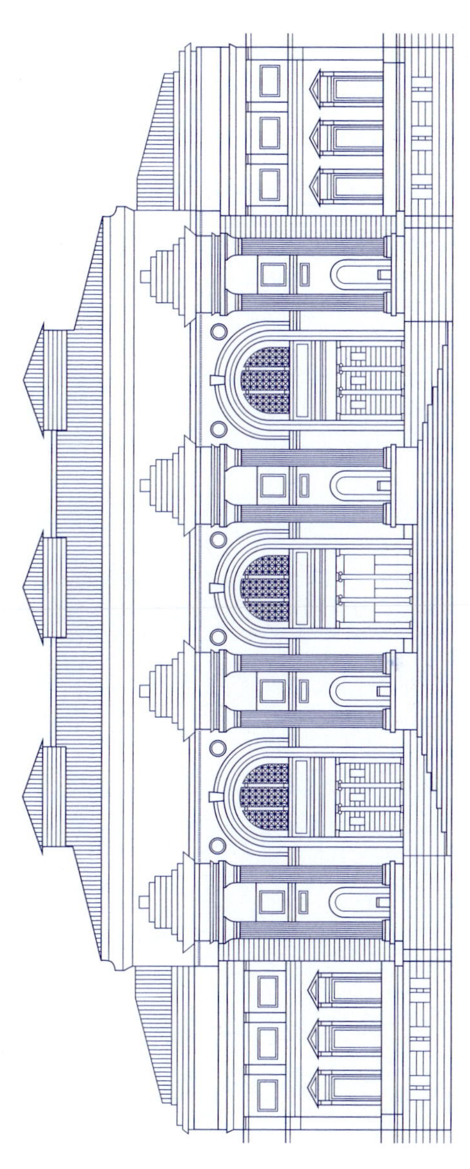

THE METROPOLITAN MUSEUM OF ART
NEW YORK

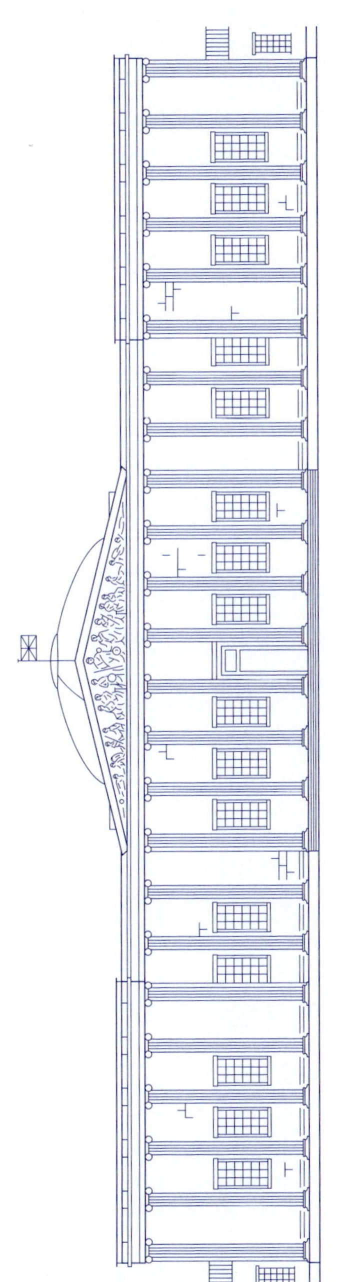

THE BRITISH MUSEUM
LONDON

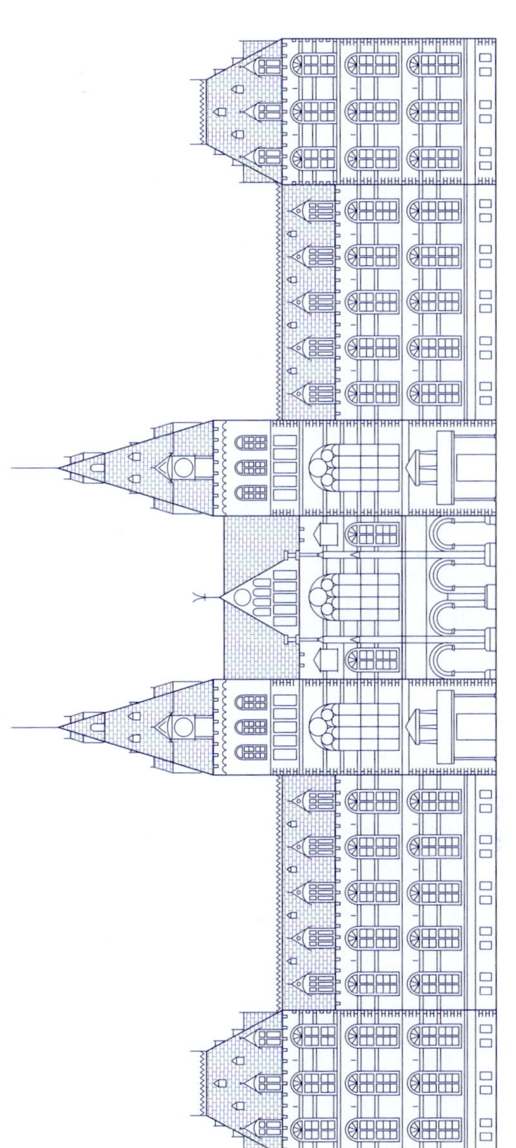

RIJKSMUSEUM
AMSTERDAM

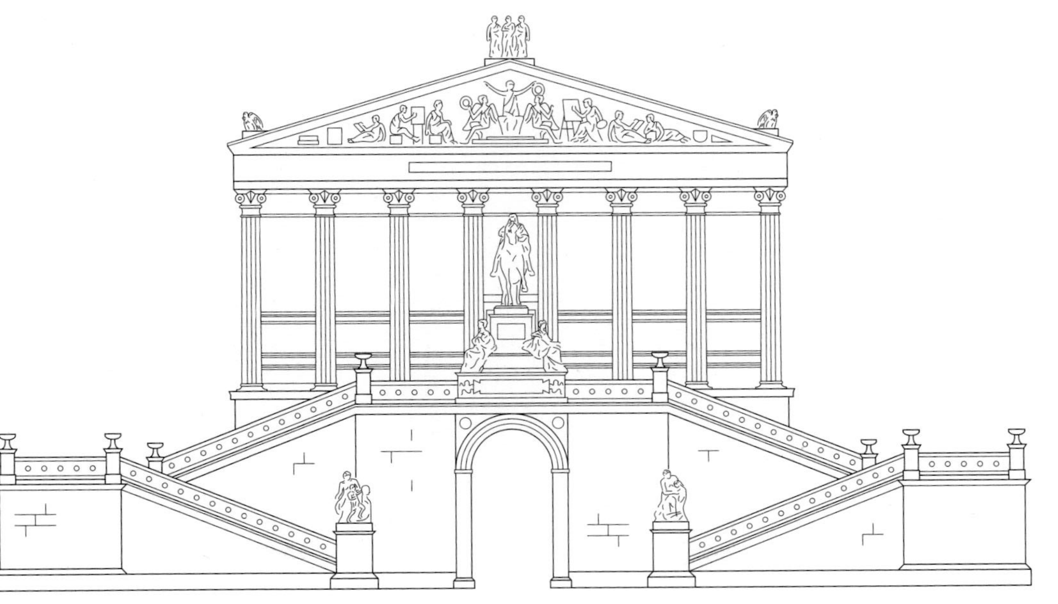

ALTE NATIONALGALERIE
BERLIN

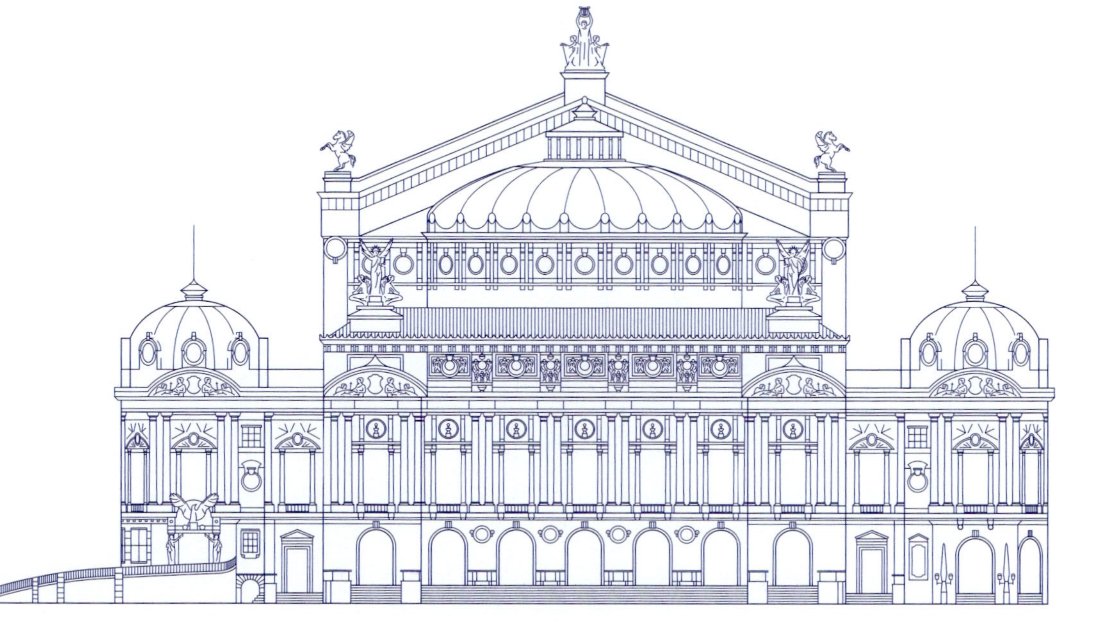

PALAIS GARNIER
PARIS

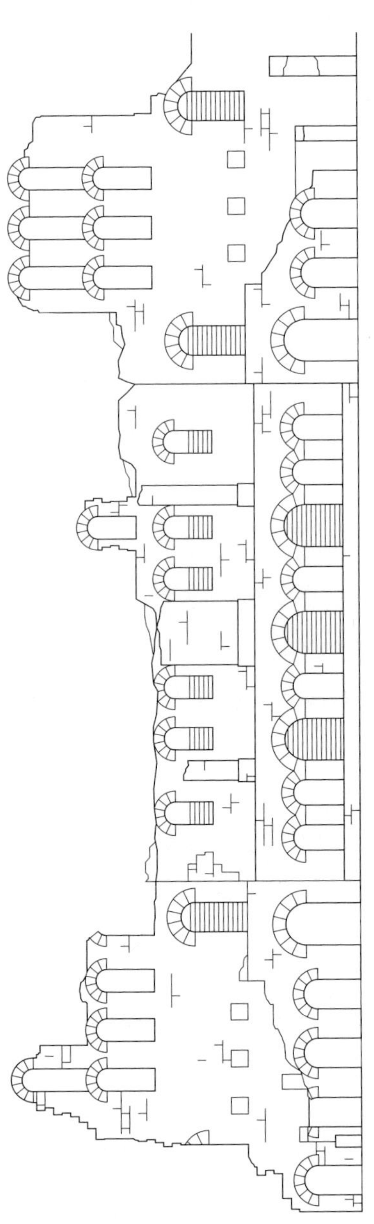

ODEON OF PERICLES
ATHENS

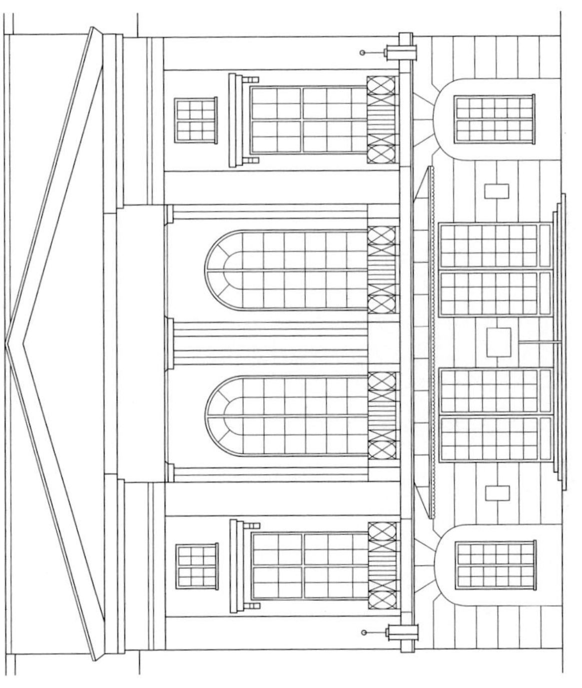

DEUTSCHES THEATER
BERLIN

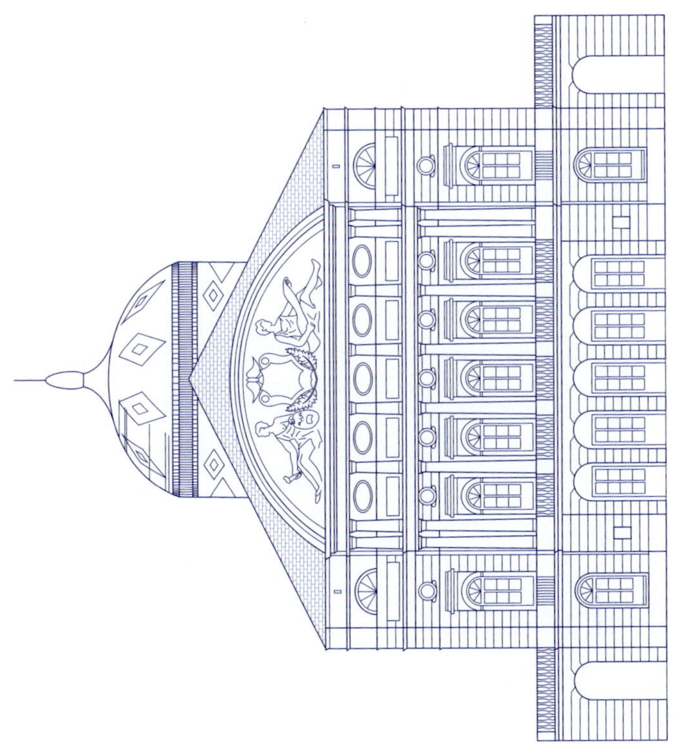

AMAZON THEATER
MANAUS

SOME REMARKS ON:
THE EXHIBITION AS A
DRAMATIC CONSTRUCTION

Among the responses to a perceived need for museums
to allow more interactivity between audiences and works
of art—which, it is believed, will necessarily lead to better
conformance with new ideals of the "inclusive" museum—
is the adoption of performance within the institution.

Curating performance in visual-art contexts is
becoming more and more popular: major institutions in the
United States and Europe now have performance departments,
collecting and archiving procedures are changing to
accommodate this development, and organizations such
as Performa are expanding into ever-wider arenas. There are
now even college and university courses devoted to the
specificities of curating performance within the museum
or gallery space.

Performance art as a category has been recognized
and acknowledged, and has become as much a part of
the general museum-going experience today as painting,
sculpture, or photography. This is an interesting development,
but within it there is a danger of setting up a false binary
between visual art and performance art. There has been
a long history of artists moving back and forth between
performance and more traditional, object-based practices.
Take, for example, the Constructivist movement and its
determination to explore life between objects, people, and
new modes of thinking about the world based on action
rather than contemplation. Kazimir Malevich and El Lissitzky,
known for their work in painting and sculpture, also founded
a collective (UNOVIS), producing ballets, operas, and plays.
Lissitzky's *Demonstration Room* and his famous *Abstract Cabinet*

were installed in the Landesmuseum Hannover from 1926 to 1927, in collaboration with the visionary curator Alexander Dorner. The display included two-dimensional works by Lissitzky, Oskar Schlemmer, and Louis Marcoussis within a kinetic installation in which audience members could move the walls to transform their viewing environment at will; Lissitzky famously called these rooms the "station where one changes from painting to architecture."[29]

Many artists today continue to work with performance as part of their broader visual-arts practice. I do not necessarily see a distinct trend toward the increased relevance of performance in the broader field of art. It has always been relevant. What is new is the drive to categorize or "curate" performance.

Curators often seek out types of art that fit into certain preconditioned aesthetics or timely trends. When Alfred H. Barr Jr., the art historian and founding director of New York's Museum of Modern Art, visited the Soviet Union in 1927, he wrote in his diary about a visit to Aleksander Rodchenko's studio: "R. showed us an appalling variety of things—suprematist paintings [...] woodcuts, linoleum cuts, posters, book designs, photographs, kino set, etc. etc. He has done no painting since 1922, devoting himself to the photographic arts of which he is a master. [... It was] an excellent evening—but I must find some painters if possible."[30] Barr was on a mission to find work that would illustrate his ideal of an avant-garde art form that rested on abstract painting, and no other medium would do.

In conversations with colleagues, I frequently discover that they are seeking a very particular type of work or a certain type of artist for an exhibition. I also find that performance for them is roughly what painting was for Barr in the 1920s. Performance art, even before it is seen or experienced in the museum or gallery, is often considered cutting edge simply because it is ephemeral and sometimes participatory.

It is also undeniable that recent mega-exhibitions devoted to performance-based works by major art stars like Marina Abramović or Matthew Barney respond to the growing imperative to put on even bigger blockbusters to generate crowds, publicity, and revenue. But huge blockbusters do not necessarily serve the work or the artists any more than they enhance the experience for the audience. They tend to gloss over the surface without launching into a truly deep investigation—it is a tragic lost opportunity. These exhibitions are usually about the creation of celebrity, the spectacle of architecture, and the canonization of particular artists, genres, and curators.

SOME REMARKS ON:
THE MAKING OF AN EXHIBITION
(OR THREE)

I generate what I call "the exhibition as a dramatic construction" through three main elements.

My particular kind of dramaturgy is always based on a text or other source material as a reference point. I keep this source material in mind as I develop all of the components of the show, from the objects in the exhibition to the exhibition design and catalogue.

I liken the exhibition to a stage set in which narrative elements unfold as one walks through the exhibition. This relates to the source material, which usually incorporates some aspect of a journey or a rite of passage.

I combine archival and nonart materials into my exhibitions to break the narrative or the viewer's immersion and pleasure, and to create a kind of estrangement or subjectivity, which Brecht and Piscator also produced in their work.

An excellent illustration of how this plays out in my curatorial work is through a trilogy of exhibitions I curated at the CCA Wattis Institute for Contemporary Arts, San Francisco: "The Wizard of Oz" (2008), "Moby-Dick" (2009), and "Huckleberry Finn" (2010).[31]

I had recently moved to the United States to take up position as director of the Wattis Institute, and the country's history and culture had always deeply intrigued me. Place and history are important for my exhibitions as all my shows respond to the sites and the context in which they happen. Exhibitions are anthropological endeavors in their own contexts.

I decided that I wanted to make a series of exhibitions devoted to seminal works in American literature. The selection of the books came about from both intellectual and personal criteria. I wanted to think about works of literature that had particular richness and resonance in American culture and history, and would be significant for me, the artists involved in the exhibition, and the audience. The three books, in addition to their crucial place in the American literary canon and the larger public consciousness, share a number of elements that have a particular relationship to the making of exhibitions. They all describe a journey, be it Dorothy's trip along the yellow brick road, Ishmael's expedition on the Atlantic Ocean, or Huck's voyage down the Mississippi River. These journeys can be understood as (and indeed were intended by their authors to function as) metaphors for human intellectual and emotional growth.

Likewise, each exhibition was designed as a journey, with a clear point of departure and very distinct "chapters." To conceive of an exhibition as a journey, as a passage through unfamiliar territories, makes particular sense when one considers how artists, just like authors, try to explore previously unknown places, not only geographically but also artistically. All three books relate to something archetypal (and archetypally American): exploration, new frontiers, overcoming adversity. *The Wonderful Wizard of Oz* is perhaps the most lighthearted of the three, but even it was intended to serve as a political allegory, critiquing economic injustices prevalent in the early years of the twentieth century, provoking serious debate at the time of its publication. *Moby-Dick; or The Whale*, with its strong metaphysical—even supernatural—bent and its multitudinous metaphors and references to philosophy, religion, and history, is definitely the most complex of the three books. *Adventures of Huckleberry Finn* is without a doubt the most provocative.

All three shows contained historical artworks, a large number of newly commissioned works, and a significant body of material related to the authors' lives and careers and to the books themselves—for instance, well-known illustrations from particular editions. The arrangement of all these elements was done to ground the viewer in the original story, while periodically reintroducing the book alongside new artworks by contemporary artists. An original first edition of the book in question was situated at the entrance of the gallery where it would be the first piece encountered by viewers. All three shows examined the history and context surrounding the books via contemporaneous critical reviews and various film adaptations. In this sense, the exhibitions were extremely time-based—situated in history as well as the contemporary moment—and the juxtaposition between the two engendered a particular dynamic within the exhibition space.

"THE WIZARD OF OZ"

I like to think of L. Frank Baum's *The Wonderful Wizard of Oz* as the first truly American fairy tale. The subjects it touches on remain relevant to how we understand America and how Americans understand themselves. Childhood, friendship, fairies, mortality, machines, wishes, desire, love, magic, illusions, good, evil, home, displacement, and utopia are only a few of the concerns written between the lines of the book.

In my exhibition, artworks and artists became characters, each with an individual story to tell. Provoking us to turn away from our immediate world and enter the sphere of imagination, the artworks allowed us to see behind the "curtain" of reality, revealing it as human-made and subjective. The connections between the artworks and

the book varied in nature. Some of the participating artists
had had a long affection for the story and addressed its
themes and characters directly, while others worked more
with the general ideas that unravel in the novel and film.

Also essential to the structure of the exhibition
was the inclusion of historical artifacts and memorabilia:
a rare first edition of the book and copies of other Oz books
written by Baum; several of W. W. Denslow's original
illustrations; the rarely seen first film based on the novel,
made in 1910; the legendary ruby slippers from the 1939
movie; the unforgettable song "Somewhere over the
Rainbow"; and a number of film stills, which were displayed
just as one would place family portraits on a desk or above
a fireplace. The artifacts were presented on colored walls
representing the colors of Dorothy's journey: Kansas (gray),
Munchkin Country (blue), the Emerald City (green),
Winkie Country (yellow), and Quadling Country (red).

The juxtaposition of artifacts and artworks not only
acknowledged the impact the story has had on popular
culture, but also provoked the sense of estrangement. Viewers
became critical observers who were deliberately guided
through the galleries, continually brought away from the
artworks and back to Baum's story. The exhibition did
not seek to simulate the book but to create something new.
The straightforward structure and attention to detail in
the installation, design, and wall texts were intended to
be self-reflexive and transparent.

"MOBY-DICK"

The second exhibition in the trilogy was based
on a more markedly complex novel, *Moby-Dick*. To fully
comprehend Herman Melville's epic story would require

diving impossibly deep. The book is about much more than its narrator, Ishmael, or we as readers, could entirely grasp. To understand Melville's sea of life requires resisting the temptation to narrow *Moby-Dick* down to a single political or metaphysical narrative: brutal tyranny, human obsession, the romance of the sea, or (worst and most reductive) a simple hunting adventure tale. Although these are certainly important elements of the story, to explore the full breadth of Melville's masterpiece one must also embrace its artistic beauty, its poetic and at times excessive language, and its deliberate, open-ended universality.

Moby-Dick is daunting, immense … and challenging to translate into an exhibition. The artworks were of course essential to the presentation at the Wattis, but equally important was the form in which the story was told. The overall structure of the show was inspired by the three-volume edition of *Moby-Dick*, published in 1930 by Lakeside Press, as well as the narrative arc of a classic three-act play. Act one, "Loomings," was the exposition, introducing us to the protagonists and outlining the dramatic premise. The artworks in this section of the gallery related to preparations for a trip, focusing on ships, the iconic figure of the sailor, and the romantic notion of the sea as perceived from the safe and stable position of land. Act two, "The Pacific," took us out onto the ocean. The mood was darker and increasingly mysterious. Act three, "The Chase," contained the final, dramatic encounter with the whale, followed by a short moment of calm and a return to a state of balance. In addition, each of the acts/gallery spaces focused in particular on one of three main characters in the book: Ishmael, Ahab, and Moby-Dick, respectively.

All of these components reflected many of the novel's most important themes and issues: religion and faith; obsession, death, and defeat; race, class, and social status;

60

friendship; homosexuality; absurdity; utopia; and, of course, humanity. In a similar vein to the exhibition "The Wizard of Oz," some artworks illustrated particular scenes and characters from the book, while others were open to a more universal interpretation. All had connections to the story but also functioned as individual artworks. Together they created a flexible, occasionally romantic, sometimes mysterious reading of Melville's enormous tale, which could be entered into from various directions and points of view. Visitors were able to immerse themselves in the story, while simultaneously acknowledging that it is ultimately impossible to fully encompass all aspects of this complex novel.

The exhibition also showcased a large number of well-known illustrations Rockwell Kent made for the Lakeside Press edition and they formed the core around which the exhibition was constructed, bringing viewers back to the original story again and again. To reflect on the all-encompassing nature of the book it seemed crucial to move beyond the concept of a display purely focused on artworks, and to integrate elements of history, anthropology, and the larger sphere of cultural production. Various nineteenth-century whaling artifacts such as harpoons, scrimshaw, maps, and lithographs made explicit connections to the history of whaling. A model of the famous whaling ship *Wanderer* at the entrance to the first gallery created a link to San Francisco, where the ship was at one point homeported.

"HUCKLEBERRY FINN"

I concluded the trilogy with *Huckleberry Finn*, the most political and controversial of the three novels. The third exhibition, via artifacts, films, older artworks, and a large number of newly commissioned pieces, was a distillation of issues raised by the iconic piece of literature, and had much in common with the previous two shows. But it was different in some significant ways. A stronger emphasis was placed on the author, Mark Twain, and "Huckleberry Finn" was specifically, even vehemently, organized to revolve around the character of Jim. This put focus of the show on one subject—race—instead of encouraging a more open consideration of the book's multitude of issues and narratives. Jim's struggles for liberty mirror an archetypal desire to be free—a wish shared by every human. To focus on this aspect seemed the most relevant way to look at Twain's masterpiece.

The examination of the past to talk about the present, a technique used in all three exhibitions, was inspired by Twain's authorial strategy, and thus became very explicit in this particular show. Twain's overt statement of setting the plot in an earlier historical period planted the idea for what proved to be an innovative and complex curatorial approach. Twain wrote his story between 1876 and 1883, and it was published in 1885. It is set sometime between 1835 and 1845, two or three decades before the Emancipation Proclamation and the end of the Civil War.

It quickly becomes clear that Twain's main objective is to speak about racism in the South, looking more generally at the moral confusion surrounding racism, discrimination, and intolerance. Both the book and the show thus express a desire to understand American realities by looking at some of the troubling, controversial, and decisive moments in the country's history, and their impact on the formation of American identity. The exhibition, like Twain's book, invited the viewer to think about where we stand in the face of racism and other forms of discrimination, intolerance, exploitation, and suppression in the United States and around the globe.

SOME REMARKS ON:
MAKING SENSE, OR NOT
(CONTEMPORARY CURATING)

In an attempt to understand how curatorial practice has evolved in the last few decades, I wrote the book *Show Time*.[32] It is a structured, methodical revisitation of fifty exhibitions of contemporary art from the late 1980s to today that truly changed the course of the discipline, and contributed to a more complex understanding of what exhibition making means. Many of the curators of these exhibitions belonged to an informal network emerging in the late 1990s, and included the first generation of globally active exhibition makers.

The exhibitions discussed in *Show Time*, representing the most innovative efforts by some of the most risk-taking curators, investigated social issues and post-Cold War political realities, and interrogated the sociopolitical engagement of the artists they featured. The exhibitions constructively (re)activated the potential of art to look beyond the limits of traditional art history, and what we may call the art world, to other disciplines such as theater, architecture, literature, and even science. The significance of these exhibitions lies in how they engaged with everyday experiences, reflected on globalization, and privileged the production and distribution of knowledge.

There have been several noteworthy efforts to create compendiums of important exhibitions, but they have mostly taken place in the context of art history, written by scholars with a focus on exhibitions as they relate to the oeuvre of an artist, or the evolution of an artistic movement. *Show Time* is distinct from these efforts in its essentially curatorial point of view—the shows having been selected from the perspective of someone actually working in the field. It is a fact that many of the significant exhibition makers of the recent past did not enter this field via an art history education; thus I felt that it was important to undertake an analysis of the form and function of exhibitions from a perspective more aligned with the practitioners being analyzed.

Show Time does not present the exhibitions chronologically but in thematic clusters, illustrating different forms of exhibitions that have been the most groundbreaking and relevant today. The chapter "Beyond the White Cube" explores exhibitions in public space—from traditional sculpture shows to citywide biennials to community-based, social-practice exhibitions that unfold over long periods of time. Another chapter examines projects by artists who were intervening in collections as acts of institutional critique, or treating the exhibition as an artistic medium. The book also surveys exhibitions that merged art with content from other fields such as architecture, science, and the mass media, as well as exhibitions that attempted global surveys of contemporary art and culture, including the landmark "Magiciens de la terre" (1989), and several others that developed as direct or indirect responses to it.[33] Show Time also looks at the ever-increasing role of the international art biennial, which has been crucial in forming the now-pervasive image of the roving international curator, and takes stock of exhibitions attempting to rejuvenate or even overthrow certain well-known exhibition formats: group shows, biennials, and collections. There is a chapter on exhibitions that deal with race, nationality, class, gender, and sexual orientation, and another on exhibitions that were formative to certain artist groups or affiliations, such as Nicolas Bourriaud's "Traffic" (1996), which was incredibly important to artists associated with what was subsequently termed "relational aesthetics."[34] The book ends with a look at exhibitions that reconsidered art of recent times, setting a new art-historical agenda with more consideration of female and non-Western artists, as well as formerly underrepresented art forms such as performance and conceptual work.

Because it falls outside the chronological parameters of the book, Szeemann's exhibition "When Attitudes Become Form" is not included. I felt that this show deserved closer scrutiny, as it is, for better or worse, the most discussed and celebrated contemporary art exhibition of the twentieth century. Indeed, I would argue that to examine and critique "When Attitudes Become Form" is to articulate the very criteria for success and failure in the realm of exhibition making in the contemporary era. For me, as a curator, the only appropriate way to analyze it was to make an entirely new exhibition about it—I called it "When Attitudes Became Form Become Attitudes," and it took place in 2012 at the Wattis Institute.[35]

What Szeemann was trying to accomplish in his exhibition was to pull together a loose constellation of artistic practices and approaches to understand the world— a world changed by new technologies, new politics, and the social movements of the 1960s. While none of the works were explicitly political, at least by today's criteria, the exhibition itself created the sense of witnessing a moment of change—one that would have been palpable in the post-1968 context. It was not a concise, thematic group show; perhaps the only thing the artists had in common was that they shared a commitment to radically question the artistic order of the day.

My "sequel" was conceived as a response to Szeemann's exhibition to recognize the importance of the original and its prominent place within the history of exhibitions, and at the same time update its concept and curatorial framework. While I appreciated Szeemann's spontaneity and lack of didacticism, I realized I wanted to carefully select the artists and artworks, and to meticulously plan how those works would relate to one another once installed. Furthermore, Szeemann's exhibition was culturally chauvinistic—there were no artists included from outside Western Europe and the United States and only three women. This would be utterly impossible to imagine today, and even then the show would not have been considered progressive. Globalization has probably had the most impact on the art world in recent decades, and the sheer number of continents and the balance of genders in my show reflected this social progress.

In keeping with the sequel concept, references to the 1969 exhibition (in the form of documentation and historical artifacts) were included, but in the main the show was composed of new works by more than eighty international artists who were invited to respond to the legacy of the 1969 exhibition and the myriad art forms it encompassed.

I described "When Attitudes Became Form Become Attitudes" not only as a sequel, but as a restoration (challenging ingrained assumptions about what the original show was about and reevaluating its status in the history of art), a remake (at least in part), a rejuvenation (bringing the thoughts and ideas of 1969 back to life), and a rebellion (against the way art and exhibitions are made today, with so much accompanying bureaucracy and red tape).

SOME REMARKS ON:
THE CURATOR'S DANGEROUS MIND

In 2010 I founded the journal *The Exhibitionist*, which can be summed up as "by curators, for curators." It was the first-ever journal solely dedicated to exhibition making. The iconic French journal *Cahiers du cinéma*, especially its early issues of the 1950s, was a primary inspiration; we were strongly influenced by its radicalism of thought, its critical and skeptical attitude, its well-written texts, and the way it broke with then-current conventions of thinking and writing about culture. Our admiration for its editors (who were almost all Nouvelle Vague film directors) was not only about the films they made (which succeeded to varying degrees in actually breaking with tradition), but also about their commitment to talking about film in their own language, working in their own style, avoiding convention, and championing intellectualism and criticality. Furthermore, *Cahiers du cinéma* took a strong stand behind the idea of the filmmaker as author, which, as I explained earlier, absolutely applies to exhibition making.

Among the many responses to *The Exhibitionist* has been one we certainly anticipated: the journal advocates approaches that put too much emphasis on the curator, to the detriment of the artist. But our understanding of curatorial practice as a form of authorship is *not* a claim that this is the *only* legitimate form of exhibition making. Rather, it is part of a larger effort to encourage the diversification of exhibition models through a focus on the subjectivity of their creators.

The Exhibitionist is fully in favor of the exhibition as the central medium of curatorial practice, as opposed to conferences, publications, educational activities, and other modes of "curating without art." Yet it also takes the stance that exhibitions do not necessarily need to revolve around art—especially contemporary art—but rather that it is highly desirable to widen the scope of curatorial examinations by including objects from the larger cultural sphere. This particular approach allows for the creation of more meaningful relationships between past and present, art and society, cultural and political history.

What is really at the core of the fear that the curator is superseding the artist? Interestingly, this critique is voiced less by artists and more by curators who claim to be merely the enablers of artists' visions and see themselves as administrators, producers, or intermediaries. This position refuses the very rich possibilities found in both art making and exhibition making. To romanticize the artist as a creative genius who requires a horde of facilitators to help execute his or her artistic vision seems shortsighted; so does the idea that curatorial endeavors must respond—after the fact, so to speak—to what artists are producing. This mind-set carries with it the implication that artists are creatively and intellectually superior not only to curators but to pretty much everyone else. There are as many untalented artists as there are untalented curators, untalented writers, or untalented cooks.

I agree that some curators have taken on a more active role in the art system—at times to an overbearing degree— yet the majority of curators are not "stars" and work on a rather less-prominent platform. I also do not share the fear that the sovereignty of artists is in danger. After all, artists can continue making work without curators, whereas curators cannot curate without artworks.

I would hope that any artist who participated in an exhibition and felt diminished by the curatorial approach would speak up and challenge the curator. In fact, the relationship between artist(s) and curator(s) ought to be complex and varied. It should change from exhibition to exhibition, from curator to curator, from artist to artist. It is too easy (perhaps even cowardly or belittling to artists) to figure that a strong curatorial voice will automatically overshadow artistic voices. Both should pull at the same end of the rope, developing arguments through dialogue to create a fruitful and nourishing relationship.

Neither art making nor curating is what it used to be. To reduce the relationship between artist and curator to a simple antagonistic binary, an enduring conflict and power struggle, is at best outdated and at worst outright reactionary. The professions have developed a form of codependency that is undeniable and mutually beneficial. Think of practitioners such as Seth Siegelaub who have taken on every role that ever existed in the art world, from gallery owner to publisher, curator, artist, writer, and so on. Or more recently someone like the curator, writer, and artist Matthew Higgs. Both Siegelaub and Higgs deliberately work against established roles and think of themselves as multitaskers. *Siloed* art-world definitions are not important to them at all.

It is also a fact that the emancipation of curating would never have happened without artistic concepts and strategies. Breaking free from the political power structures of museums and other large art institutions, curators have clearly learned from artists, appropriating strategies from institutional critique and from 1960s and '70s Conceptual art. Such appropriations have created a closer relationship between artists and curators, and a more visible involvement of artists in curatorial practice. The issue of authorship brings artists and curators together again because more and more art emerges out of a conscious confrontation with its own history. In any field, a crucial way to push forward is by challenging, questioning, and examining the standards of the past. Take for example the famous Armory Show in 1913, organized by American painters Walt Kuhn and Arthur B. Davies, which introduced European avant-garde art to the United States, included Marcel Duchamp's controversial *Nude Descending a Staircase.*

By taking everyday objects into the exhibition context, Duchamp's readymades not only radically transformed the way we think about art but also changed the way we think about making exhibitions. Duchamp's famous *Fountain,* for example, which he submitted to the exhibition organized by the Society of Independent Artists in 1917, was refused despite the fact the society was supposed to accept all members' submissions. In protest, Duchamp and Walter Conrad Arensburg, who were both on the board, resigned immediately. Think about it: when Duchamp made it clear that any object exhibited in an exhibition could potentially be a work of art, he was radically uncovering the mechanisms of the exhibition context and the power of exhibitions.

SOME REMARKS ON:
A REQUISITE RECALIBRATION
OF THE CURATORIAL

Another impetus behind the founding of *The Exhibitionist* was to create a consistent platform or forum for regular, interconnected conversations that would bring together the many fragments of current curatorial dialogue. One measure of the vitality of a discipline is the intensity of the debate surrounding it, and curatorial practice has enjoyed a massive intensification in this respect over the last decade—including the foundation of numerous academic programs, the creation of conferences, and the publication of an increasing number of specialized books. Generally, I feel that most of this discussion has not been productive or coherent, nor has it truly pushed the discipline forward.

Curating is a relatively young field with a short history. It certainly borrows from the more established disciplines of art history and cultural studies, but it is still in its adolescence, still transitioning from an open, creative, largely undefined practice to a diverse professional arena with many highly specialized branches. I fear these specialized branches are producing mountains of discourse that will bury or suffocate many essential thoughts.

Many existing publications on curating profess to offer an overview of the field as it exists today, or attempt to map its historical trajectory. Others propose a series of case studies under a common curatorial theme. Some compile the collected writings or interviews of a single curator. All are hoping to contribute to this relatively new discipline, and its accompanying canon, by putting forth a shared set of values and a knowledge base.

But how basic is this knowledge base? In an attempt
to redefine what it even means to go back to the basics,
I commissioned a series of essays in 2011 and 2012 titled
Ten Fundamental Questions of Curating, which were published
in *Mousse* magazine and later collected into a single volume.[36]
For this series I invited ten international curators to address
an essential issue in the field they felt others had missed,
ignored, or deemed already answered. The series aspired
to offer a real critique of existing publications and modes
of thinking. The writing was extremely sophisticated but
the intent was a bit tongue-in-cheek—a return to a kind
of zero-degree state—at a time when a recalibration of what
a curator is and does seemed both necessary and urgent.

SOME REMARKS ON:
THE UBIQUITOUS AND STRANGELY
HOMOGENEOUS BIENNIAL

A key finding in the research behind *Show Time* was
that the group exhibition has become *the* vehicle for creative
expression as authored by an exhibition maker. This strand
was not really identified before—at least not consciously
on the part of curators. Since the postmodern crises of the
1980s, curators have become much more aware of their
voices and authorial roles in making exhibitions, and more
self-conscious in relation to the field of curating as a whole.
As curating became a creative act in its own right, the group
show became the favored medium. Other identifiable trends
have included a greater emphasis on large-scale thematic or
historical group exhibitions, an increase of overview shows
with emerging artists, and the explosion of the biennial.

The evolution of the large-scale international biennial
is certainly one of the biggest innovations in exhibition
making since the 1990s. Among the most admirable and
radical examples is Manifesta, the nomadic European
biennial, whose recent iterations have been more and more
concerned with European politics: immigration, deindustrial-
ization, and Europe's relationships with its neighbors in
Africa and the Middle East. Manifesta started in Rotterdam
in 1997, and has since involved numerous curators from
all corners of Europe. Through this expansion, art from a
number of previously marginal contexts has been introduced
to a wider audience.

While the globalization of the art world had already
begun in the 1980s, albeit at a much slower pace, it was
still possible to possess some comprehensive understanding
of most of the current trajectories in art. The art world had

only a limited number of centers, and many of today's art hubs, including London, São Paulo, Warsaw, Los Angeles, Mexico City, Shanghai, and Berlin, played only very marginal roles. Until the discourses of postcolonial theory and identity politics arrived in the curatorial offices of museums, it was unusual to see art made by artists from outside Western Europe or North America.

A number of museum exhibitions started to change this situation—most famously the Centre Pompidou with "Magiciens de la terre." But it was mainly biennials and other international group exhibitions, such as the documenta editions of 1997 and 2002, that offered an overview of artworks from around the world on a significant scale. Biennials started to appear (Sydney, Gwangju, Istanbul, Johannesburg, and many locations in the former Eastern bloc), specifically took up issues of globalization and postcolonial discourse, and happened in places that had formerly been on the periphery, establishing them as go-to destinations for globe-trotting contemporary art aficionados, while also offering an international overview of art (based on the Venice Biennale model with its national pavilions). This format was immediately copied (but simultaneously questioned) and is only now starting to be seriously reexamined.

There is surprisingly little diversity in the curation of biennials today. Most have a distinctly "spectacular" aspect and, one could argue, a sameness in their specific language and form. They are simply global overviews, presenting what is going on around the world in the sphere of contemporary art at a given time under some vague theme. Most biennials in the United States focus myopically on art from just a few cities, usually New York and Los Angeles.

I have curated several biennials that have taken wildly varied forms, depending on the contexts in which they were staged. I have already mentioned the 12th Istanbul Biennial in which my cocurator and I sought to identify ways of broadening and challenging the formal and theoretical vocabulary of the standard biennial to reassess how politics and aesthetics are articulated in contemporary art and represented in exhibitions. We wanted to encourage visitors to become active readers, not just silent recipients.

And then there was the People's Biennial I cocurated with Harrell Fletcher. It was a unique collaboration between an exhibition maker and an artist who share a similarly critical yet optimistic outlook on the art world. It was a traveling exhibition presented between 2010 and 2012 at five art institutions in the United States: the Cantor Fitzgerald Gallery at Haverford College, Pennsylvania; the Scottsdale Museum of Contemporary Art, Arizona; the Southeastern Center for Contemporary Art in Winston-Salem, North Carolina; the Dahl Arts Center in Rapid City, South Dakota; and the Portland Institute for Contemporary Art, Oregon. The venues were geographically distant from one another, and also from mainstream art centers, which for us was crucial.[37]

The show consisted of contemporary works by five to ten artists from local communities in each city. Fletcher and I visited each community for up to a week, conducted research, lectured, held roundtable discussions with local artists, and finally selected the artists and works to be featured. We exclusively showed work by artists who never had significant exposure, thus offering a potential model for more community-based exhibitions. In appearing grassroots, even amateurish, the People's Biennial called explicit attention to how most so-called professional art is merely art that conforms to a set of conventions most of

us have accepted and internalized. It used typical display
techniques but with a subversive intent: to set up a feeling
of familiarity in the viewer that was then shattered by
the unorthodox artworks on view—again that sense of
estrangement. The goal was to present art as immediate,
spontaneous, vulnerable—and not as it is often presented
in other biennials: distant, conceited, calculated.

As with all biennials, there was controversy about
who was invited to participate and who was not. A number
of artists in the communities we visited felt uneasy about
our decision to include lesser-known artists, as they'd hoped
our project was an alternative biennial or anti-biennial that
would finally give them some wider visibility. The more
established the local art scene, the harsher their reactions
were toward our ideas. More than once we were accused
of having created the People's Biennial as a way to promote
ourselves rather than the invited artists. Fletcher and I enjoyed
fielding these objections and discussing our project publicly
while we were doing our research, because all parts of the
process helped us to precisely articulate what we were after.

Another aspect of the globalization of the art world over the past few decades was the emergence of the so-called independent curator who organizes worldwide exhibitions and curates biennials. Names such as Hou Hanru, Okwui Enwezor, Hans Ulrich Obrist, or Rosa Martínez come to mind (Martínez alone curated or cocurated more than ten biennials in the last ten years!). It is a position still idealized by many. Although the idea of an independent curator may appeal in terms of the professed freedom and flexibility, many independent curators of the 1990s, such as Maria Lind, Barbara Vanderlinden, Dan Cameron, Maria Hlavajova, Robert Fleck, Ute Meta Bauer, Mary Jane Jacob, Vasif Kortun, Charles Esche, Francesco Bonami, or Yuko Hasegawa, among others, were in fact never really independent; most worked in museums in junior positions or as adjunct curators, ran small art centers, or taught at art schools. If they were truly independent, this was often not because they wanted to be but simply because they could not find a job in an institution. The economic realties of being an independent curator without a permanent affiliation with a school or museum never allowed for more than a small number of individuals to actually make a living.

For many curators from the so-called periphery of the art world, such as Asia, Africa, or South America, it became possible to work as independent or semi-affiliated curators in the "center" by using specific art knowledge from their native countries, and by curating shows in a still largely Western-dominated context. This apparent success was also accompanied by some restrictions, and curators from those regions who began operating in the 1990s were often branded as "the Asian curator," "the African curator," or "the South American curator," and were utilized accordingly and perhaps unimaginatively.

The 1990s also saw the emergence of a number of curatorial innovations through the work of several (independent) curators longing for a change of the established norms and rules of exhibitions. A diversification of exhibition models started to appear that not only took on theoretical models and discourses but also brought more creativity to the understanding of what an exhibition could be. All of these curatorial initiatives and changes arguably resulted in the increase in educational curatorial programs during the last ten years and thereby placed the curator, at least temporarily, into the spotlight of the art world.

While the 1990s was the decade of the independent curator, the new millennium saw many of these former independent curators moving into institutions and bringing along their often unorthodox ways of working, thereby changing the programming of exhibition spaces across Europe. This development became known as "New Institutionalism," established by art centers in the early 2000s such as Garanti Contemporary Art Center in Istanbul (run by Vasif Kortun, 2001–10); Rooseum in Malmö (run by Charles Esche, 2000–03); Palais de Tokyo in Paris (run by Nicolas Bourriaud and Jérôme Sans, 1999–2006); the Kunstverein in Munich (run by Maria Lind, 2002–04), and in Frankfurt (run by Nicolaus Schafhausen, 1999–2005), to mention a few. All of these art centers, with their different ideas and strategies, began to move away from traditional institutional practices and proposed less exhibition-based and more process and discourse-oriented curatorial strategies.

Although most of the above-mentioned institutions are no longer run by these directors today, the initial impulse for change remains as the backbone of these spaces and has led to the establishment of new forms of institutional programming in Europe. Charles Esche once described the role of the Rooseum (which permanently closed its doors in early 2006) as that of an "active space," a hybrid structure that was part art school, part community center, and part artistic laboratory. In a more recent development, a number of prominent curators have moved away from working in art institutions entirely, making educational institutions their temporary home—for example, Okwui Enwezor was the dean of the San Francisco Art Institute (2005–09); Russell Ferguson was the chair of the Department of Art at the University of California in Los Angeles (2006–13); Ute Meta Bauer was the associate professor of the Visual Arts Program at the Massachusetts Institute of Technology in Cambridge (2005–13); Maria Lind was }the director of the Center for Curatorial Studies at Bard College in New York (2008–10); Saskia Bos as the dean of the School of Art at Cooper Union in New York (2005–present); or Daniel Birnbaum, who was director of the Städelschule in Frankfurt (2001–10), immediately followed by Nikolaus Hirsch, and then by Philippe Pirotte (2014–present).

One of the many regions "opened" to the art world during this period of expansion and transformation was the former Eastern bloc. After 1989 this area contributed seismic changes to the art world. The wall came down and we had a whole new part of the world to look at for art. The western canon was challenged. The biennial that specifically looked to integrate Eastern European art into a Western context was Manifesta.

During the past decade a number of major museums
have begun to focus on global expansions, building new
facilities and extensions to make art more of a mass cultural
event. They have also implicitly tried to fundraise by loaning
"curatorial expertise" and their collections to museums
or cities (for example, the Guggenheim often does this).
In the 1990s the biennial was the tool for putting a
previously marginalized city or region on the cultural map,
whereas the focus of the new millennium has been on the
design of new museums and extensions by international
"star" architects. The so-called Bilbao effect is still a desirable
model for many cities to revitalize their communities.
The impact the opening of Tate Modern had on the art world
cannot be underestimated. With five million visitors per
year and endless coverage in mainstream newspapers,
it opened the door to a totally new way to encounter art,
and is a success story that most other museums dream of.
Yet it is interesting to note that during this time many art
institutions lost a great deal of their power and influence;
only a handful of sites dominate the institutional scene or
can have an impact on the career of an artist. Most museums
must now compete with biennials or even commercial
galleries in order to secure the attention of artists.

With the emergence of a connected and truly
international art world, a global art market emerged during
the late 1990s and the early years of the twenty-first century.
It has had, and continues to have, a number of severe
consequences. Contemporary art fairs are starting to replace
the experience of seeing art in a museum as more and more
people only see art in a commercial context—at auctions,
fairs, and commercial galleries. The borders are further
blurred when large commercial galleries hire museum
curators and (with their seemingly endless resources)

produce museum-quality exhibitions and publications. Auction houses have lately come more to the fore, threatening galleries as the primary dealers of contemporary art, and one wonders if the competition posed by auction houses and art fairs might be the beginning of the end for traditional gallery operations. In addition, many so-called centers for contemporary art rarely serve as hubs for art and artists working outside art market considerations. Places situated outside of the mainstream have emerged as the true centers of the art world because of the concentration of artists living there and the absence of a dominating (and dictating) market influence.

Proliferation and expansion characterize the post-millennium art world and have created a range of disorienting effects, including a fragmentation of intellectual and artistic discourses and the disintegration and breakup of what was, until a few decades ago, a relatively homo-genous artistic environment. The art world has grown as a result of a number of interrelated events that occurred over the last decade or two—rapid cultural and economic globalization being the most significant cause for change.

SOME REMARKS ON:
THE CONTINUED NECESSITY
OF MAKING EXHIBITIONS

Looking at the visual-art context today, it is becoming
more difficult to form a coherent argument or position.
Most participants in the art world are simply trying to handle
the enormous amount of information (found in books,
articles, invitations) received every day. The inability to digest
this proliferation of information means that many practitioners work within their own niche discourse.

Is it still possible to recognize innovation? And can
curation have a larger impact if it is robbed of its inventive
qualities before it can propose something new—silenced
through the process by which visual art identifies otherness
as an essential part of what feeds its continuation? We can
only hope that true innovation will find its way to the
surface no matter how complex or difficult the conditions
of today's art world really are.

It is impossible for any field to truly progress without
understanding its own past. All of the radical expansions and
redefinitions in curatorial work have triggered much reflection.
The many conferences, books, articles, and graduate programs
devoted to curatorial studies are all part of an inevitable
self-referential impulse—a desire to understand where the
field of curating comes from and where it is heading.

I strongly believe that anyone working in any
intellectual field should, every few years, review the essential
questions of their practice and reflect on their relationship
to it. Curatorial innovation, new theories of curating, and
critical discourse should be welcomed and encouraged. But
the new and fashionable should not distract us from engaging
and reengaging with what we already think we know.

Over the course of my career I have repeatedly asked myself questions addressed in *Ten Fundamental Questions of Curating*. I believe it is necessary to interrogate the simplest, most basic principles of one's own profession, precisely because the answers are simultaneously quite complex and almost never given any thought by others. In the case of curating: What is a curator? What is an exhibition? Whom do we curate for? These questions are so straight-forward, so fundamental, that most curators bypass them entirely. They take the answers for granted, assuming the relevance of curatorial work in the wider world, thereby indulging in a dangerous sort of unchecked, assumed self-importance.

I assert that curators are in a uniquely situated position that can help find answers to the key questions of humanity—and to simultaneously pose new questions. To suggest this reflects a certain tendency in our latest understanding of curating and exhibition making, in which curatorial operations and modes of inquiry come closer to the field of anthropology than to that of art history.

Curators should ideally be curious and inquisitive human beings. They must feel compelled to wrestle with, study, and analyze essential questions of the human condition. And since these questions relate not only to the production of culture but also to the creation of histories and even reality itself, curators should consider themselves as operating outside the borders and the confines of traditional academic modes of inquiry.

What are some of these key questions of humanity? There are the truly essential questions about our origins (Where do we come from?), epistemology (How do we know what we know?), or ontology (Who are we, and what is our reality?). And then there are more advanced questions related to aesthetics (What is beauty?), ethics (What is wrong and what is right?), ecology, religion, and power.

Humanity and culture are unstable categories. They are multifaceted and constantly being negotiated; their definitions are evolving and dynamic. As concepts they exemplify orderly chaos. The role of curators should be about bringing order into this chaos through the creation of culture. Curators should develop strategies to examine and select objects that will be exhibited in a gallery space and to offer a particular theoretical argument. These arguments are possible interpretations of how we could go about asking and answering essential questions.

Curators—alongside philosophers, anthropologists, archaeologists, ethnographers, and so on—are involved in the study of how humans have constructed realities, asked questions, and created culture and civilization. The ultimate goal of all this is to understand ourselves more thoroughly and apply our findings and our creations. We must not forget that we are makers as well as researchers—helping to improve humanity.

ENDNOTES

1   Marshall McLuhan and Quentin Fiore, *The Medium Is the Massage* (1967; repr., New York: Penguin Books, 2008), 132–36.

2   Rosalind Krauss, "Sculpture in the Expanded Field," *October* 8 (Spring 1979): 30–44.

3   Arthur C. Danto, "The End of Art: A Philosophical Defense," *History and Theory* 37, no. 4 (December 1998): 127–43.

4   Hans Belting, *The End of the History of Art?* (Chicago: University of Chicago Press, 1987).

5   David Joselit, *After Art* (Princeton, NJ: Princeton University Press, 2012).

6   Rasheed Araeen, *Art Beyond Art: Ecoaesthetics, a Manifesto for the 21st Century* (London: Third Text Publications, 2011).

7   "; c/k ; curatorial / knowledge phd research program," program website, Goldsmiths, University of London, http://ck.kein.org/.

8   documenta X, artistic director Catherine David, held in Kassel, Germany, June 21–September 28, 1997.

9   documenta XI, artistic director Okwui Enwezor, held in Kassel, June 8–September 15, 2002.

10 "Nowhere," organized by Lars Nitve, was held at the Louisiana Museum, Humlebæk, Denmark, May 15–September 8, 1996.

11 Since 1993, "Do It" has been presented in at least fifty different locations worldwide. See Hans Ulrich Obrist, ed., *Do It: The Compendium* (New York: Independent Curators International; Distributed Art Publishers, 2013); "En Mas' do it," Independent Curators International website, http://curatorsintl.org/special-projects/do-it.

12 Joseph Kosuth, "The Play of the Unmentionable," Brooklyn Museum, New York, September 27–December 31, 1990.

13 Fred Wilson, "Mining the Museum," Maryland Historical Society, Baltimore, April 4, 1992–February 28, 1993.

14 "David Hammons: The Unauthorized Retrospective," was held at Triple Candie, New York, January 8–February 12, 2006; "Cady Noland Approximately: Sculpture and Editions, 1984–2000," was also held at Triple Candie, New York, April 20–May 21, 2006.

15 Ydessa Hendeles's "The Teddy Bear Project" was first presented as
part of the exhibition "sameDIFFERENCE," held at the Ydessa Hendeles
Art Foundation, Toronto, March 9, 2002–May 16, 2003. It was
subsequently featured in "Partners," at the Haus der Kunst, Munich,
November 7, 2003–February 15, 2004, and then in "Noah's Ark,"
at the National Gallery of Canada, Ottawa, June 1–October 3, 2004.
"The Teddy Bear Project" was last remounted as part of the 8th
Gwangju Biennale, "10,000 Lives," September 3–November 7, 2010;
"Predators and Prey (The Zeppelin Project)," 2002–05, was held
at the Ydessa Hendeles Art Foundation, Toronto, May 2006;
and "Dead! Dead! Dead!" was held at the Ydessa Hendeles Art
Foundation, Toronto, May 2007.

16 Philippe Parreno, "Anywhere, Anywhere Out of the World,"
Palais de Tokyo, Paris, October 23, 2013–January 12, 2014.

17 Maria Ley-Piscator, as quoted in *A Dictionary of the Avant-Gardes*,
ed. Richard Kostelanetz, 2nd ed. (New York: Routledge, 2001), 481.

18 Maria Ley-Piscator, *The Piscator Experiment: The Political Theatre*
(New York: J. H. Heineman, 1967), 14.

19 Herbert Marcuse, *The Aesthetic Dimension: Toward A Critique of
Marxist Aesthetics* (Boston: Beacon Press, 1978).

20 Marcuse, quoted in Douglas Kellner, *Herbert Marcuse and the Crisis
of Marxism* (Berkeley: University of California Press, 1984), 357.

21 Marcuse, quoted in Carol Becker, *Zones of Contention: Essays on Art,
Institutions, Gender, and Anxiety* (Albany: State University of New York
Press, 1996), 46.

22 Leo Kerz, "Brecht and Piscator," *Educational Theatre Journal* 20, no. 3
(October 1968): 364.

23 Untitled (12th Istanbul Biennial), organized by Jens Hoffmann and
Adriano Pedrosa, September 17–November 13, 2011.

24 Félix González-Torres, interview by Robert Nickas, "Felix Gonzalez-
Torres: All the Time in the World," *Flash Art International* (January–
February 2006): 90–94 (ill).

25 François Truffaut, "Une certain tendance du cinéma français,"
Cahiers du cinema 6, no. 31 (January 1954): 15–29. Reprinted in English
as "A Certain Tendency of French Cinema," in *Movies and Methods*,
ed. Bill Nichols (Berkeley: University of California Press, 1976),
and in *Cahiers du cinéma in English*, no. 1 (January 1966): 36–41.

26 Roland Barthes, "The Death of the Author" (1967), reprinted
in *Image, Music, Text*, trans. Stephen Heath (New York: Hill & Wang,
1977), 142–48.

27 Michel Foucault, "What Is an Author?," presented to the Societé
Français de philosophie on February 22, 1969, and reprinted in
Aesthetics, Method, and Epistemology, ed. James D. Faubion (New York:
The New Press, 1998), 221.

28 "Live in Your Head: When Attitudes Become Form (Works–Concepts–
Processes–Situations–Information)," organized by Harald Szeemann
and held at Kunsthalle Bern, March 22–April 23, 1969.

29 El Lissitzky, *El Lissitzky: Life, Letters, Texts*, ed. Sophie Lissitzky-Küppers
(Greenwich, CT: New York Graphic Society, 1968), 325.

30 Alfred H. Barr Jr., "Russian Diary, 1927–28," in Soviet Revolutionary
Culture, *October* 7 (Winter 1978): 21.

31 "The Wizard of Oz," September 2–December 13, 2008; "Moby-Dick,"
September 22–December 12, 2009; "Huckleberry Finn," September 28–
December 11, 2010. All curated by Jens Hoffmann and held at the CCA
Wattis Institute for Contemporary Arts, San Francisco.

32 Jens Hoffmann, *Show Time: The 50 Most Influential Exhibitions of
Contemporary Art* (London: Thames & Hudson, 2014).

33 "Magiciens de la terre" was curated by Jean-Hubert Martin and held
at the Centre Georges Pompidou and the Grande Halle de la Villette,
Paris, May 18–August 14, 1989.

34 "Traffic" was curated by Nicolas Bourriaud and held at CAPC Musée
d'Art Contemporain de Bordeaux, January 26–March 24, 1996.

35 "When Attitudes Became Form Become Attitudes" was curated by
Jens Hoffmann and held at the CCA Wattis Institute for Contemporary
Arts, San Francisco, September 13–December 1, 2012.

36 Jens Hoffmann, ed., *Ten Fundamental Questions of Curating* (Milan:
Mousse Publishing; Stromboli: Fiorucci Art Trust, 2013).

37 The People's Biennial, curated by Jens Hoffmann and Harrell Fletcher, was
presented at: Cantor Fitzgerald Gallery, Haverford College, Haverford, PA,
January 27–March 2, 2012; Southeastern Center for Contemporary Art,
Winston-Salem, NC, July 8–September 18, 2011; Scottsdale Museum of
Contemporary Art, Scottsdale, AZ, June 23, 2011–January 15, 2012; Dahl
Arts Center, Rapid City, SD, January 14–March 27, 2011; Portland Institute
for Contemporary Art, Portland, OR, September 10–October 17, 2010.

THEATER OF EXHIBITIONS
JENS HOFFMANN

Published by Sternberg Press

Copyeditor: Niamh Dunphy
Proofreader: Lilah Leopold
Design and illustrations: A Practice for Everyday Life
Printing: BUD Potsdam

Typeset in Joanna by Eric Gill,
"a book-face free from all fancy business."

ISBN 978-3-95679-087-4

Sternberg Press
Caroline Schneider
Karl-Marx-Allee 78
D-10243 Berlin
www.sternberg-press.com